When *they* Choose Change

A Four Step Process to Guiding People through Change

By

Roxanne Sawatzky

ISBN-13: 978-1502508300

ISBN-10: 1502508303

Printed in the United States of America by CreateSpace

Bulk purchases, please contact empoweringchange@mymts.net

Website: empoweringchange.ca

Dedicated to those who taught me that lasting change comes from within.

Table of Contents

Forward

When *they* Choose Change is a book based on almost ten years of formal research projects that I have been a part of, where we explore the question: What moves ambivalent individuals forward? This book is also greatly influenced by the diverse people I have worked with over the last twenty years.

I have always been fascinated by change. My desire to see change began long before my "paid" career did. I remember at the age of ten changing my parents living room around (pictures included). The vision of what could be drove me to drag and heave that heavy couch across the room. At the age of twelve I began my "private client practice". Once again the vision of what could be kept me busy trying to improve the lives of my brother, friends and even teachers. What I soon discovered is I couldn't make anyone change, regardless of the vision I had for them. What those early days did for me was to plant a seed. The seeds were thoughts that desired an answer to the question: If we can't "make" people change regardless of how wonderful the change could be, than what does?

It is no surprise to me or those close to me that I completed my M.A. in Organizational Change. My education background is in Addictions, however, I quickly moved into the employment sector, specifically working with individuals who experience barriers to employment. My research focus has been in the employment sector as well, specifically with people who are reluctant to enter or re-enter the Labour Market.

What I have learned over my lifetime, regardless of education level, or socio-economic background is that people get "stuck" and the only effective way to see them move forward is When *they* Choose Change. It is my hope that this book will be a great resource to you regardless if you are a parent, practitioner, or leader. The process for working through ambivalence is the same, always being mindful that *they* must choose to change. I wish you great success!

7

Introduction

There are two things that we encounter in life that are inevitable; at some point in your life's journey, you will find yourself faced with these two things: the call for change, and feelings of ambivalence associated with those changes.

Perhaps you yourself are going through a situation that necessitates changes and this brings about inner feelings of conflict or uncertainty. Or perhaps you are a practitioner, helping to guide clients through changes and their feelings of ambivalence. Or maybe you are a leader attempting to ease the uncertainties of your employees during the transitional period that comes along with an organizational change such as a merger or deployment of a modernized, state-of-the-art computer system. (Think merger, or new computer system!).

Regardless of the types of changes you are currently faced with, despite the magnitude of these changes, there are tried-and-true methods that have been developed for making change (and the ambivalent feelings that so often accompany it) easier. Note that we did not say, "easy"—but eas*ier*.

Within this book, I will discuss strategies that have been used by a variety of professionals that I have trained in guiding others through change and resolving ambivalence. If you are a service provider trying to guide the people you serve towards specific behavioural changes, or a leader trying to help your organization steer through diverse emotions related to workplace changes, you are not alone. If you are looking for guidance as you navigate through the challenges of change and question whether it is possible to actually *influence* said change then I invite you to please read on. The strategies to accomplish these goals lie within.

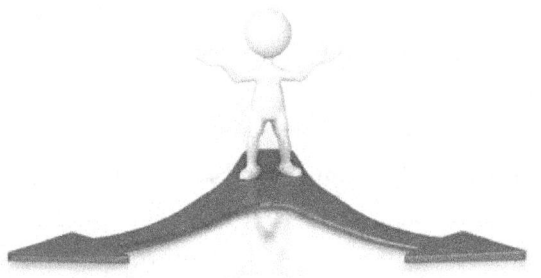

Ambivalence

What is *ambivalence*? The Merriam-Webster dictionary gives a threefold definition of this word: "simultaneous and contradictory attitudes or feelings (as attraction and repulsion) toward an object, person, or action," as well as "continual fluctuation (as between one thing and its opposite)," and "uncertainty as to which approach to follow." No matter which definition of the word is applicable in any given circumstance, each of the three definitions has one thing in common: the theme of conflict, juxtaposition, and being "torn between." We will briefly explore this inner conflict in this book, but before we do this keep in mind that, while you may believe people are in denial about changing, or that they are intentionally digging their heels in, it is likely not the case. Although it may appear that way to an outside observer, this is not necessarily the case. In fact, people often feel two ways about change—they are caught up in ambivalence—and for the time being, they are choosing to stick with the status quo (not to change). Fortunately, we can influence this.

We like to think of the space between not changing and changing as ambivalence. When someone feels ambivalent about something, he or she is caught up in uncertainty due to feeling two incongruent ways about that change. While these steps were originally created for service providers who work with ambivalent clients and for leaders who want to support organizational change, they truly serve as a guide to exploring and resolving ambivalence for anyone.

The steps in this book are intended as a strategy to help you guide the ambivalent person as he or she explores his or her own motivations and to help him or her discover the impetus for behaviour change through insight and self-exploration. The bottom line is that we want behaviour change to come intrinsically, from the person's own will, rather than from some external force. While an external force can be the stimulus for change, our hope is that both external and internal reasons will line up at some point and the individual can *choose* what path he or she will ultimately take. For those who desire to see someone make a behaviour change, this book will guide you as you wrestle with the temptation to nudge or even push someone towards change and instead will assist you to draw out an intrinsic motivation, no matter how small that motivation may be.

We begin the process of exploring and resolving ambivalence by setting our intention to listening in order to understand the individual's dilemma, thereby creating a space wherein the person may be open to considering change. While it may make perfect sense to us that someone *should* change, it's never quite that easy in reality. Change is complex, and not a black and white process. Often we don't realize ourselves why we resist change. When we begin a discussion with someone about a dilemma or about making a change, you want to determine if change is important to this individual and if so, *how* important?

Resisting the urge to follow our own inner voices

I would also encourage you to be aware of how important it is to *you,* that the individual make a change. The more pressure we feel to see someone change, the more likely we will try to problem solve and remove barriers for that person. There is this fantastic video on Youtube: *It's not About the Nail.* In the video a woman has a nail in her forehead; she is talking with her partner about the pain she is experiencing in her forehead and how all her sweaters are snagged. When her partner suggests she remove the nail, she becomes frustrated and reminds her partner that it's not about the nail plus she doesn't want him to fix things!

This video does a great job at illustrating that, while *we* think it's about the nail or the barriers it really isn't—not to the individual in question. We must be aware of the importance *we* have for the person to change, and in so doing, keep that importance of ours in check. We also want to recognize that when we are working with an individual who is ambivalent, it is possible for a leader or practitioner (even one with the best intentions!) to get in the way of someone successfully transitioning through change. Peter Senge (2006) introduces us to *mental models*; he describes mental models as assumptions, beliefs and images. Unfortunately, our mental models (or our assumptions about the way things were, are, or should be) can often lead us down the wrong path. For instance, we may assume we know why someone is "stuck" (ambivalent), and not only do we presume to know why he or she is stuck, we might also believe we know what he or she needs to do to move forward! Drs. Miller and Rollnick talk about the *righting reflex* in their book Motivating Interviewing, Motivating People to Change (2013). This reflex is a desire to "fix," and to come up with solutions as our inner voice tells us that surely the reason the person is stuck is because they lack information—information that *we* would be happy to give them.

> *"I believe that it is an increasingly common pattern in our culture for each one of us to believe, every other person must feel and think and believe the same as I do. We find it very hard to permit...[others] to feel differently than we do about particular issues or problems. Yet, it has come to seem to me that this separateness of individuals, the right of each individual to utilize his experience in his way and to discover his own meanings in it, - this is one of the most priceless potentialities in life".* Carl Rogers

This desire to provide information is a common roadblock and rarely effective when we encounter someone wrestling with ambivalence. You see, most people already have plenty of information or at the very least they know how to get the information once they are ready to change.

So, why do we feel compelled to provide information? When a person is experiencing ambivalence, it is common to hear him or her say, "I would like [or need] to change, but…." The righting reflex—our desire to fix— often compels us to provide information or find solutions for this person in a quest to be helpful to him or her. Add our assumptions to the mix and we have a recipe for disaster. What we have done is whittled ambivalence down to someone simply lacking the know-how to change. Or, if the ambivalent (stuck) individual does not heed our suggestions, we in turn deem this person difficult, in denial, or simply unmotivated—when in fact, this may not be the case at all. As mentioned earlier, the person may feel two different ways about the proposed change and at the moment the status quo is winning out—and in truth, we don't like it, and want to fix what we perceive as problematic. And why do we feel this way? Because of the assumptions that comprise our mental models and the sway of the righting reflex. Withholding our opinions and resisting the righting reflex can be the most difficult part of resolving ambivalence.

Imagine, if you will, someone who is considering having a baby. A woman—we'll call her Mary—comes to see me because she never imagined being a parent, however, that may change. Mary states, that she never really saw herself as a mother while growing up. She could envision working at a job she was passionate about and being in a loving relationship, but being a mother? Not so much. That changed, however, when she met Pete. When Mary and Pete fell in love, marriage felt like the next step in their relationship. That was, until Pete shared his desire to have a family. As a result, Mary discovered that she was feeling ambivalence with regard to having a child, and she knew she needed to discuss her dilemma with someone objective.

What if I, someone who is a parent, carried the belief that women should have children and should do so early in their life. To add an extra layer of assumptions what if I believed that one day our adult children will help support us as we reach old age, thereby reducing the amount of stress on the government to provide for the elderly [just to be clear, I don't actually feel this way—but let's say for the sake of this hypothetical situation that I do]. How would my beliefs and assumptions influence Mary's decision? What if I wasn't a professional who was aware of how mental models and how the righting reflex can influence the way I work with ambivalent people? I likely would—even if only subconsciously—push her in my covert mission to direct her toward a decision: that having children is the only way to go! After all, she wasn't sure what to do and I, being objective (hardly!), can surely offer her some support.

In fact, the more I push Mary toward my ideas, the more she will move toward the status quo, whether consciously or unconsciously. After all, someone has to defend the other side; it looks like it will have to be her since I disregarded it completely in my attempt to bolster my own agenda. It's not easy to curb the desire to fix.

Sometimes, when people have been in the "system" for a while, the fight or desire to defend the status quo (let alone consider change) has died out. I have heard a few clients say: "you ask me some questions, I answer, and I get what I need." Then, sadly, the cycle begins once again. It's as though we practitioners and clients are set in a pattern to oscillate; like a rocking chair we just keep going back and forth. In his book, *The Path of Least Resistance*, author Robert Fritz describes this phenomenon of oscillation. He wrote that "if you are in a structure that leads to oscillation, no solution will help. This is because these psychological solutions do not address the structure, but rather the behaviour that comes from the structure." Fritz (1989) is not implying that all your approaches are ineffective, he instead is saying that our solutions or approaches are temporary, at best.

What we want is a structure or system that focuses on *intrinsic* change, where the desire to change comes from within—as it should. At this level, the client is no longer oscillating. Instead, the individuals' intrinsic motivation propels them forward towards change. First however, we need to change the way we work with those who are caught up in a state of ambivalence.

I believe clients long to be heard, to know and be known, and that we are all a part of a very complex and broken system. Clients have told me they no longer want to be the mouse in the cage—where they are examined, questioned and fixed. They want something to be different, as do we all. Unless we change our approach, I think clients will continue to disengage and we all will suffer for it. I have heard numerous practitioners cling to their outdated methods and state that it's the clients fault; they say "the person never wanted to change anyway." This serves to further convince them that they are right—after all, their approach worked for the dozen other clients they have worked with. This may be true, but one must consider other factors that may have come into play in those situations where the approach appeared to be successful. What stage of readiness were the other clients in? If an individual is *ready* for change, you are simply a stepping stone along their journey towards their goal.

Furthermore, what if the client who didn't respond to the "fixing" practitioner wanted and needed a different approach—but didn't have the words to say so? One of my favorite quotes offers us great insight into the client's world: "…and sometimes I have kept my feelings to myself, because I could find no language to describe them" (Jane Austen, *Sense and Sensibility*).

What we all need to remember is that people want and crave the space to explore their ambivalence without judgment. They want to be able to hear their own inner voices and to be understood internally as well as externally. When working with an individual who is ambivalent, it is important to create this space for the person, so that he or she can explore what exactly it is that keeps them "stuck". While there may be barriers to making a change that we can easily see, *that* discussion—the discussion of barriers and possible ways to overcome them—comes later in the conversation. First, there needs to be resolve and commitment to change. Once you have this, you would then be able to focus on the barriers—if any still exist after the ambivalence is resolved.

Things to remember:

- Ambivalence is not about lacking information, it is about feeling two ways about an issue

- Assumptions can influence the way you interact with people – be aware of this and do your best to suspend judgment
- Resisting the righting reflex can be the hardest part of resolving ambivalence

Building a strong foundation of engagement will serve you well when discussing change. Engaging the person you are working with by creating a space for someone to explore their dilemma without judgment or pressure to change is the best gift you can give. If you are reading this book and find yourself ambivalent about making a change, you may recognize that those around you have plenty of advice on how you can and should change. While their advice may be well-intended, you might find yourself resisting their suggestions. That's normal. At this early point in exploring and resolving ambivalence, information or advice may not necessarily be what you need. Soon you can evaluate the advice you are being bombarded with. But first, let's take a step back and answer the question: how important is it to make this change?

Importance

With the righting reflex and assumptions firmly in check, a good place to begin is by exploring how important it is for someone to change. In other words, exploring the individual's own perception of the importance of the proposed change as it relates to his or her life.

I like to use *Rollnick's rulers* (from Motivational Interviewing methodology) to explore importance to change, and I will refer to them often within this book. Rollnick's rulers (also referred to as "change rulers") are subjective measurement tools; they are scales that range from zero to 10 which are used to gauge feelings about change.

Imagine, if you will, a ruler in front of you: the ruler begins at zero and ends at 10. Our first step is to begin at zero and work our way toward 10. As with all rulers, this one begins at zero. In this instance, zero represents no behaviour change (or the status quo) and 10 represents behaviour change. Note: the key goal here is beginning at zero and working toward 10—if we jump ahead, you will soon find yourself in a wrestling match when instead you want a dance. Be patient, put your dancing shoes on, and first determine how important this change is to the individual you are working with.

The conversation can begin like this: "On a scale of zero to 10, how important would you say it is for you to stop collecting government assistance?" Or, "How important is it for you to implement this new process in our department?" If the individual states that the proposed change is highly important to them (by rating it a six or higher), you are off to a good start. If the proposed change is *not* very important to the person (rated five or under), you might want to ask what could increase the importance of making this change. Asking this question will give you an indication of the person's values.

The individual's values are one of the most important components of resolving ambivalence. This is a concept which we will explore later in this book. For now, it will be helpful for you to understand that we want to give the ambivalent person an opportunity to consider how import the proposed change is to them. Let's assume the person indicates the importance to change is an eight. In such a case, we want to *affirm* that this change is important to them and you would like to hear more about why. Exploring the "why" allows the person to clearly identify what has meaning to them; on some levels the person knows the obvious reasons or the "why" for changing. While the individual may be aware of why he or she moves the ship toward the lighthouse, what is missing or confusing is the understanding of why he or she doesn't have his or her oars rowing in the direction of those values that the lighthouse represents.

The face of ambivalence

If someone is "stuck," sometimes we need to take a step back and look at the reasons to *not* change—not always, but sometimes. The challenge for all of us is being clear on when it makes sense to ask the person for the reasons to not change, i.e., when the person should keep his or her boat docked on shore. We will do our best to help guide you in knowing when it makes sense to explore the reasons to not change; sometimes however, you must trust your intuition and have the confidence that what the individual needs most is to give voice to his or her reasons for not changing (or, conversely, to focus only on the reasons *to* change). At this point, being open to exploring the benefits of staying the same is enough.

 As mentioned, there are times we begin our conversation by exploring the benefits of *not* changing. Mostly, I would explore the reasons to not change when I am in a place of equipoise. Equipoise is a balanced approach that strives for equilibrium rather than attempting to sway the situation toward a particular outcome. This is where you are intentional about *not* being directional towards change but instead allow the ambivalent person to determine if changing has more value than staying the same.

There is a temptation to begin with (or move the conversation to) why a person wants to make a change. While this approach of exploring reasons to make behaviour changes makes perfect logical sense, it isn't always the most effective way to resolve ambivalence. Remember, we want to maintain a state of equipoise. So, instead of exploring what *could be*, we want to create a space where we can acknowledge what *is*—in other words, creating a space to explore the positive aspects of maintaining the status quo and *not* changing.

If you are working in an organization as a service provider that *mandates* behaviour change, you likely are *not* in equipoise. If this is the case, you don't want to explore the benefits of the status quo—or at the very least, you want to be careful not to linger on the benefits of not changing. When I am working with someone who has been mandated to change (for example, by finding employment or not using any illegal substances), I usually skip this step and move directly into exploring what reasons the individual has to change. However, you cannot completely dismiss the fact that that there are reasons that a person is not changing. You will notice those reasons to remain in the status quo will continue to pop up throughout the discussion. When they do, you want to acknowledge what you heard in an empathic and patient way—and while you acknowledge what you have heard, you don't linger within these barriers (reasons to not change).

That said, if I am working in a situation where someone is not mandated to change and they simply feel ambivalent about the prospect of changing, I definitely recommend taking the time to explore the benefits of not changing. Knowing that when someone is ambivalent, he or she feels two conflicting ways about change, you are naturally inclined to explore the benefits of changing—and soon, you will—but first you may need to begin with Step 1.

The most important thing to remember is that the individual must be allowed to make the decision for him or herself. Anytime you feel tempted to actively "fix" or go into problem-solving mode, you have forfeited the process and will run up against resistance or disengagement on the part of the individual.

> "The more I am open to the realities in me and in the other person, the less do I find myself wishing to rush in to "fix things". As I try to listen to myself and the experiencing going on in me, and the more I try to extend that same listening attitude to another person, the more respect I feel for the complex process of life. So I become less and less inclined to hurry in to fix things, to set goals, to mold people, to manipulate and push them in the way that I would like them to go. I am much more content simply to be myself and to let another person be himself". Carl Rogers

Some resistance on the part of the "stuck" individual is to be expected, at least initially, and resistance can take many forms: being argumentative and aggressive, minimization and being dismissive, going off on unrelated tangents or ignoring questions completely, or worse – disengagement. Resistance is the individual's way of expressing that he or she is on a different wavelength than you. It is a way of expressing that he or she does not feel heard, and does not feel understood. Continued resistance can lead to disengagement (the individual giving up on the conversation), and this is why *accurate empathy* on your part is of the utmost importance. We will discuss the concept of accurate empathy in greater detail later in the book.

A Four-Step Guide to through Ambivalence

When trying to help guide an ambivalent individual out of what sometimes feels like swamp, it can be difficult to know where to begin. There are four steps that you can use to help someone step out of the swamp of ambivalence and step up to accepting and even embracing change—whether it's an inevitable change outside the individual's control (such as a merger or deployment of a new software system company-wide) or a change that must be initiated from within the individual (such as the decision to start job hunting in hopes of living a life without the help of public assistance programs). Before we explore approaches you can use I would encourage you to consider the conditions necessary for growth. Carl Roger's notes, acceptance, empathy, and positive regard are the necessary conditions for growth, while you move through a relatively linear approach, people however, are not linear, nor are conversations, be mindful to create conditions for growth and remain flexible throughout your discussions.

This chapter serves as an overview of these four steps, which will be explored in greater detail in the chapters to come. Let's briefly discuss each step so that you can familiarize yourself with them before putting them to use in your own situation:

Step 1: Benefits of staying the same

It may come as a surprise that, when we are guiding someone through the process of change, we suggest discussing the benefits of staying in the status quo. However, this is the first step in the ambivalence resolution process, especially when you are in a position of equipoise. As I mentioned earlier, when I am *not* in a position of equipoise there are times that I will explore the reasons to not change, but when I do this I am mindful to not linger here; I simply acknowledge there are reasons to not change and ask what those might be. When we explore the benefits of staying the same we are at a zero on our ruler. Until we move on to Step 2, we haven't moved yet toward behaviour change.

So often an individual wants to embrace a change, yet has reservations about it—the status quo, after all is the norm; it is a comfortable place that the person is already accustomed to. The status quo is business as usual. Although an individual may recognize that change is beneficial and have a desire to go with the flow of the change, it can be very hard for an ambivalent individual to do this.

Here's the thing: part of why the status quo is hard for ambivalent people to let go of is that the status quo has, in some way, become unacceptable. Staying the same is presented as a bad option (by company leadership enforcing a change and wishing everyone would let go of the past and get on board with the new and better way, for example—or by the individual's support network trying to aggressively steer the individual toward change and away from the status quo). Maintaining the status quo is viewed by some as being so undesirable that it doesn't warrant any sort of discussion whatsoever—a sort of "perish the thought" approach. This way of doing things, however, can be counterproductive. Sometimes, all the ambivalent person needs to get the ball of change rolling along is an outlet—permission to acknowledge the benefits of the status quo. For this reason, we suggest giving the ambivalent individuals you work with a safe place where they can do just that, free of judgment.

Step 2: Benefits of embracing change
The next step involves moving on from discussion of the status quo to discussing the benefits to embracing the proposed change about which the individual feels so ambivalent. Acknowledging the positive things that would come along with the change is an important part of helping the individual to see that this change is not a scary, intimidating thing that is to be procrastinated or avoided, but rather, a thing which could have a remarkably positive influence on his or her life. By steering the conversation in this direction, you give the ambivalent person a chance to state the benefits of changing aloud, which can be immensely helpful in sparking the inner desire to change, and in turning confusion and uncertainty into a more firmly cemented resolve to roll with the change. Now that have begun exploring the benefits of change, we are moving

towards behaviour change. We would likely be around a five or six by the end of this step. I will describe later in the book how we move from zero to five while in this step.

Step 3: Building confidence

The third step in the process is building the individual's confidence. Much of the time, a person has a desire to be receptive to change but doesn't feel capable of making the change—he or she doesn't feel self-assured because he or she has low confidence in the ability to change. This is where we come in. By using the suggestions within this book, you can help the ambivalent individual to build his or her confidence up to a level that makes moving toward change a real possibility rather than a far-away dream. An individual may inwardly embrace the *idea* of change, but when he or she lacks belief in his or her ability to effect that change, the individual stays stuck in the mire of the swamp of ambivalence. Once a person finally builds sufficient confidence to feel equal to the task of change, he or she can at last begin to plan for ways to make it happen. In this step, we are somewhere around a five or six on the ruler, with the intention of moving to an eight or nine.

Step 4: Making the commitment

The final step in the process takes everything out of the cognitive realm and puts it into the tangible realm—that is, we turn our attention from thinking and talking about change to actually going out there and *doing* it. In this step, the individual is encouraged to make an action plan which outlines a change-related goal. The individual can then carefully break this goal down into specific steps to take in order to accomplish it, and can finally start to act on this desire to change. The individual can then report back to you if they desire about his or her progress with regard to reaching the goal he or she had set. They can also debrief any hurdles faced during the process or relapses into old behaviour and how they can move forward. This step is the culmination of all your efforts—it is the thing that finally leads you and your clients or staff out of the swamp of ambivalence once and for all. Finally, in this step we are at a nine or 10 on the behavioural change ruler, at the place where you or the individual has described actual steps that can be taken toward the desired change.

Four Steps

When trying to help guide an ambivalent individual, it can be difficult to know where to begin. The following are skills that can be used when exploring the Four Steps which will offer you a guide to navigating a way through ambivalence—not past it, not around it, but *through* it. We would encourage you to use *micro-skills*, which include *open-ended questions, affirmations, reflections*.

Open-ended questions
When having a conversation with an ambivalent person, it is important to keep the line of questioning open-ended. Rather than offering options as one would with a multiple-choice quiz, it is better to ask questions in such a way as to encourage the individual to ruminate and expound. This encourages deeper and more critical thinking on the part of the ambivalent individual, and leads the person to come to his or her own conclusions without being led there or forced to compartmentalize his or her answer according to a prescribed set of "acceptable" answers that he or she has been given. For example, asking, "What have you considered trying as a next step?" Using this approach leaves the individual an opening to come up with his or her own ideas, without feeling pushed toward or away from any particular outcome.

Affirmations
Affirmations are positively-spun statements made by the person conversing with the ambivalent individual (leadership, manager, case worker, friend—whomever is acting as the guide). These statements serve to emphasize and reaffirm the ambivalent person's strengths, and to bolster confidence by giving active and verbal recognition to moves the person has already made toward a necessary change. Rather than being empty praise, affirmations are a *true* recognition of the real steps that the individual has made toward positive behavioural change. For example, when the individual talks about a time when he or she dug deep to find inner strength and see a task through to completion against all odds, you

might comment to the effect of, "You are a very strong person who can meet the challenge when it arises...."

Reflections

Offering reflections involves mirroring what the individual has said to you in your own words. This technique allows the individual to know that he or she is being understood when he or she speaks, and it also helps you to know that you have an accurate concept of what the person is trying to tell you with his or her words. Thus, reflections serve a twofold purpose. You can also use your reflective technique to help guide the individual toward or away from a given course of action, if applicable. For example, by reflecting in an amplified manner and *overstating* your reflection, you can help the individual to back off from what he or she has stated. In contrast, by *understating* your reflection, you can help the individual to build up and intensify feelings about a given statement.

Step 1: Explore the Benefits of the Status Quo

While this step may seem odd or even counterintuitive, it provides an opportunity for the individual to hear and better understand his or her own reluctance to move forward. We encourage you to keep your opinions and ideas to yourself and demonstrate a high level of empathy as you provide this unique opportunity for the person to explore his or her reasons for not moving forward.

Questions to ask yourself

Is your position to move someone toward behaviour change? Or remain in equipoise?

As previously mentioned equipoise is where you are intentional about *not* being directional towards change but instead you allow the ambivalent person to determine if changing has more value than staying the same.

If the intention is to move someone toward changing his or her behaviour, you don't want to fully unpack this step—in other words, you would only acknowledge the reasons for not changing without exploring them in deeper detail.

A great place to begin is asking the person how important the change is to them. You can use a scaling question to find this out. For example you can ask:

How important on a scale of 0-10 with 10 being most important is it for you to make this change in the next (add a length of time). Reflect back the importance that you heard the individual share. If you hear low importance you can ask the person what could increase the importance of making this change.

Once you have discovered the importance of the change and reflected back what you heard you can ask the client to take a step back and consider what would be good about not making this change?

Optional Questions:
- What are the good things about not making this change?
- What do you think prevents you from making this change?
- What do you think gets in the way of changing?

Accurate Empathy is Key

Empathy is the ability to listen attentively to what the ambivalent individual is expressing to you, and being able to paraphrase or summarize what you heard in the most concise-yet-precise manner possible. It involves becoming a mirror of sorts, and accurately reflecting your understanding of what was shared. Your goal is to ask for each reason the person has to remain in his or her status quo situation, followed with a reflection demonstrating accurate understanding (empathy).

"If I let myself really understand another person, I might be changed by that understanding. So as I say, it is not an easy thing to permit oneself to understand an individual, to enter thoroughly and completely and emphatically into his frame of reference". Carl Rogers

If your intent is to remain neutral about the change, you would explore this step in depth with the individual. In other words you would unpack their reasons to not change. If your focus is to invite this person to move towards behaviour change you would not unpack this step and only ask and acknowledge reasons to not change.

NOTE: there are circumstances when you would bypass this step completely. If your mandate is to *encourage behaviour change*, you would proceed to Step 2 at this point.

If you have the option to *maintain a stance of neutrality*, please read on.

There are some situations where remaining neutral is more appropriate than guiding someone toward behaviour change. For example, if someone is torn between choosing one of two equally-rewarding options such as returning to school, changing careers or changing departments at work, it is likely most appropriate to remain neutral, and explore the benefits of both fields equally.

Optional Questions if you are in equipoise:

- Tell me more about this reason (1st reason offered)? Explore or "flush out" the *values* held by the individual that are attached to each reason given.
- Why is this (reason) important? This will offer you deeper insight into the individual's values.
- What about this (reason) is meaningful to you?

Step 2: Explore the Benefits of Changing

While it may be tempting to share your views on why a person should change, this step provides an opportunity for the individual to hear and offer his or her own reasons to change. This step has three components to it: the top of the iceberg, the bottom of the iceberg and creating a discrepancy. We begin at the top of the iceberg by eliciting all the person's reasons to possibly consider change.

Top of the Iceberg

Asking for the individual's reasons to change leads to discovering what importance making this change has for him or her.

Optional Questions:

- What would be the good things about making this change?
- What reasons can you think of to make this change?
- What are the main reasons you or others see for making this change?

Using your micro-skills, *affirm* and *reflect* all reasons the person shares. This demonstrates your understanding of the reasons that the individual has given. Reflecting also creates a space for the individual to hear their reasons for taking steps towards change. Often people will share that no one has given the time and space to consider their reasons to change, but instead others will tell them why they should change which encourages resistance to change.

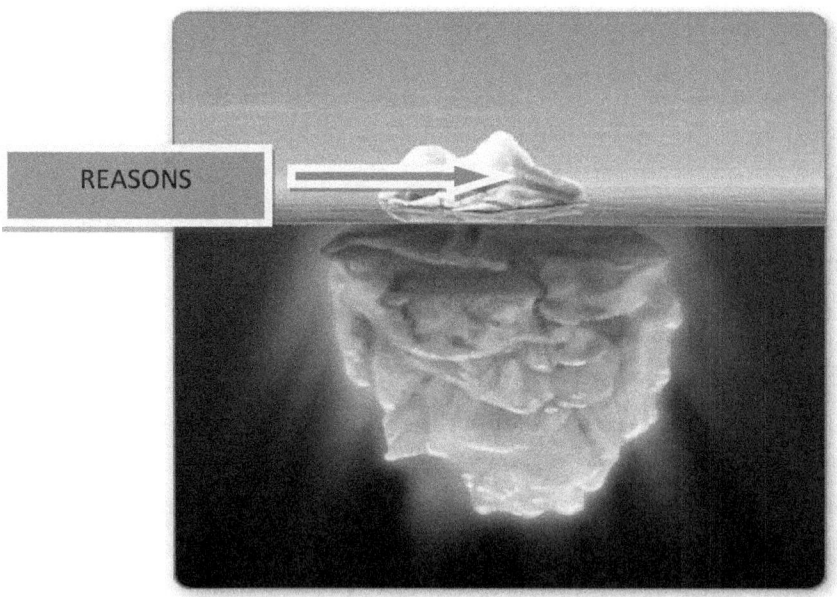

Bottom of the Iceberg

While it is certainly important for us to explore all the reasons the person has to change, we must recognize we are still at the *top* of the iceberg.

Our next move is to explore the *bottom* of the iceberg: the *"WHY."* The "WHY" = values. This is the heart of making change—we change because we want the way we behave to line up with our deeply-held values. Exploring the "WHY" will provide both you and the individual with insight into these values. This is an essential part of exploring ambivalence and change.

Unpack all the reasons – ask

When you begin to explore the *importance* of the reasons, you get to the core values that lie beneath the reasons. Discussing the significance of these reasons will lead to discovery of the individual's core values, which unlocks the door to insight. *Reflect, affirm* and *summarize* all values that the person has shared.

Optional Questions:

- "Why is this (1st reason) important?"
- Tell me more about _____?
- What are the good things about _____?

Values

When you have a deeply-held value discrepant with a current behaviour, it is likely that the behaviour will change. When a person holds two conflicting beliefs about a given topic or situation simultaneously, *cognitive dissonance* takes place. Cognitive dissonance is experienced as a sense of unease and feelings of stress over having these two beliefs which contrast one another. The individual who is ambivalent about behaviour change is caught up in cognitive dissonance—the key reason for the person's ambivalence is a conflict between the desire to change and the desire to remain complacently the same.

Create a Discrepancy

At this point the person you are working with has had the opportunity to explore their reasons and values to change. It's time to create a *discrepancy*. The purpose of creating a discrepancy is to act as a mirror for the incongruence between the person's inner voice that says what is truly important and his or her actual behaviours, a mirror where the individual can hear their heart and hope for change.

You want to create a space where the individual can see and hear the discrepancy between the deeply-held values that he or she has shared (all the information provided that was under the top of the iceberg) and his or her current behaviour.

30

Example

Carefully reflect the discrepancy with openness and without judgment by noting that "it's important to you to live a long and healthy life. Yet you are smoking two packs of cigarettes a day to deal with your stress". You can add an open question by asking the person "how does continuing to smoke line up with what's important to you?"

At this time in the conversation, the individual is likely feeling quite uncomfortable, as an actual cognitive understanding of the conflict between his or her behaviour and his or her values has been reached. This feeling cannot be maintained for a long period of time—therefore, you will want to "pull" the person through the window of ambivalence or he or she will begin to inwardly *lower the importance* of the values that he or she shared.

You are likely hearing a lot of language in favour of changing from your client at this point in the conversation. We want to focus on responding and strengthening their reasons for change. We can respond by:

- Asking the person to elaborate
- Affirming the person's values, behaviours and beliefs
- Reflecting - desire, ability, reasons and need
- Summarizing change talk and follow with an open question that will give you more change talk

It is important to proceed to Step 3 where you will focus on increasing confidence for change. This will prevent the individual from diminishing the importance of his or her values, which can happen if the person does not have the self-efficacy to change. Remember, we cannot maintain a discrepancy between our values and behaviour for long periods of time, so seize the moment!

Step 3: Increase Confidence

A common characteristic of ambivalence is high importance placed on deeply-held values being paired with low confidence to change behaviors' that are in conflict with those values. We want to focus on building the necessary confidence to follow through with desired change. There are many reasons and values to support changing; however, confidence in the ability to perform the change is low. While there may be the temptation to move into a plan of action at this time, we would encourage you to fully explore Step 3, and then work on an action plan.

Create a neuro-pathway

An important part of this step is creating a neuro-pathway—an easement of sorts for the impending behaviour change. We like to think of a neuro-pathway in the brain as files in a filing cabinet. Imagine the filing cabinet is our brain and in the cabinet we have many files (neuro-pathways). Those files are past experiences and thoughts, and these experiences and thoughts are what create a neuro-pathway.

If we don't have a file that says we made this change (the proposed change) before, that means we don't have a neuro-pathway—there is no precedent for the change, nothing to draw upon from past experience telling me that we are capable of making that particular change.

Without a neuro-pathway a common reaction will be the fight, flee or freeze response. This can be quite frustrating for an individual who *wants needs* or *has to* change but feels unable to do so as the confidence for change isn't equal to the reasons to make the change. In other words, Pete may place a high level of importance on changing, but has a low level of confidence in his ability to do so. As a result, you see no follow through and Pete remains in the status quo.

Another thing to consider with the file cabinet analogy is that a file can become corrupt—in other words, we could have already experienced this proposed change in the past, and the end result was disastrous. This makes our brain say, "HALT! This was a bad experience for us before and we don't want to go here again. Let's *not* make that change." So we choose the status quo instead, and opt to *avoid* the very change we want and have solid reasons to make. What we want to do is let the brain know that this change will be better this time around. We do this by creating a *new* neuro-pathway.

How to create a neuro-pathway

We begin by asking how confident the person is to make the proposed change. Scaling confidence provides the person with an opportunity to rate where he or she is at with his or her confidence to make the change, and what needs to be done to increase that confidence. Take your time while scaling confidence; you can elicit a lot of information and steadily see the individuals' confidence increase as you work through this area.

Ask:

"Joe, how confident are you (on a scale of zero to 10, with zero being low and 10 being high) that you can initiate this new change?' Joe responds with a three. Follow this up by asking Joe what he would need to increase his confidence in his ability to change in the next month from a three to a four. Notice that I *quantified* my question: this is important. I could have said, "Joe, how confident are you that you can make this change?" His response would likely be very different if I had left that question too broad and open-ended. By quantifying the question, you will get an accurate idea of where Joe is at with his ability to make this change and what he needs in order to increase his confidence and actually make the change successfully.

Continue to ask "what else" he needs to increase his confidence in the next month. I prefer to write all the responses down on a desk flipchart so that he can see for himself what it would require for him to move forward.

You will note that by scaling up, I find out what Joe will need to move forward. After Joe states that he has nothing else to offer, I would return to my original question and scale down, thus finding out what strengths Joe has.

Ask:

"Joe, what gives you the confidence of a three on the scale and not a zero?" Joe responds by saying: "I have had to find work in the past and was able to do so and I know I can do it again." Affirm all the strengths you hear the individual state. This is an important part of increasing the confidence to change. I continue to ask for all the reasons Joe is a three and not a zero and affirm each response.

Ask for past successes
If the person can elicit a recollection of a past positive change experience, the brain is likely to bypass that fight, flee and freeze response and become open to considering the proposed change in a less fatalistic light. It can determine that, *"Perhaps this change won't be so bad; I experienced change before and I was successful, so maybe I can experience another new change without disastrous consequences, after all. I lived and possibly even thrived through change in the past and I can do it again."*

Begin by saying:

- "Think of a time in the past when you didn't think you could make a change—but you did, *and* you were successful." Ask for two past examples. By asking this question you are providing the individual an opportunity to see that he or she has indeed experienced change before and it had a positive outcome. This serves to boost confidence by unveiling capability based on past successes—if it worked before, there isn't any reason that it couldn't work this time, as well.

Explore internal and external strengths
Sometimes, when you ask people about what strengths they have they may respond by saying, "none." Try not to let this initial response discourage you. To increase the individual's confidence you want to explore internal and external strengths that can be tapped into in order to make this change. The target in Step 3 is all about increasing confidence for the proposed change. Self-efficacy is one's own level of belief in oneself—how capable a person feels, how *able* someone sees him or herself when it comes to accomplishing goals and "getting the job done"—whatever "the job" may be. Self-efficacy, then, is a measure of one's *perceived* ability to rise to life's challenges.

Ask:

"Tell me about some of your internal and external strengths. For example, I may say that I am stubborn—otherwise known to me as 'determined." We recommend looking at both internal strengths and external strengths. An example of an external strength could be having a driver's license. Another example might be the high level of respect from the community or an organization where someone volunteered. This is where we find out what people think they "have going for them." This is a way of determining the individual's self-efficacy.

Supports

While self-efficacy is important in making changes, so is having the support needed to carry out those changes. Sometimes mountains feel too difficult to climb alone. Similarly, the thought of making a difficult change may simply be too much to cope with without the help of others.

Ask:

"Who can offer you support as you consider this change? In what way could this person be a support for you? How would you go about asking for support?"

Envisioning
When we create a *specific* neuro-pathway for the desired change, we do so by envisioning the future change. Ask the individual to imagine how he or she would get from A to Z with this specific change.

Example:

We might ask: "When you consider returning to work after recovering from this injury, how might you do it?" Another example might be: "When you consider finding employment, what do you think the first step would be?"

If the person can't visualize the next step (by *looking forward*), we would shift the discussion to the perspective of *looking back* and say: "Imagine that you made this change successfully, and now it's six months after the fact. How did you go about it? What was the first step?" Continue through each step.

By slicing each step into small, bite-size pieces, we can create a clear neuro-pathway for change.

I fully encourage you to be collaborative through this step. If you have ideas, now is the time to share them. I would recommend sharing your ideas by asking for permission first. After the person has shared his or her ideas, you can ask if you can offer some suggestions for consideration.

Step 4: Elicit a Commitment and create an action plan

There is a very good chance that you are near the end of resolving ambivalence to change. We have worked with the individual on identifying reasons to not change, with a high level of empathy. We explored reasons to change and expanded on those reasons by finding the values attached to making the proposed change. We also created a neuro-pathway to make the change.

Finally, we want to elicit a commitment and determine what the next step is for the individual. We do this by paying close attention to the language we hear.

Optional Questions:

- What do you intend to do?
- What would you be willing to try?
- What is one small thing you could do to move towards change?

Listen for use of commitment language
"I will," "I plan," "I intend."

These phrases are *commitment language*—language used by people who are open to making a change and are making solid plans that they wish to follow through with. You know that people who use commitment language are likely to move towards behaviour change. If you hear what

Motivational Interviewing pioneers Drs. Miller and Rollnick refer to as *change talk* (see below), then you will want to reschedule another meeting for a future date and time. This allows the person to process the steps and the conversation that you have had together. If you have good momentum, you can carry on with the conversation, but be mindful that sometimes people need some time to reflect upon and process this rich discussion they just had with you. One reason that a person might continuously use change talk without actually advancing toward commitment is the *timing* of the change. For example, the individual may feel that they need to do XYZ, but first he or she needs to do some research or have a discussion with someone else—and that's OK, too. Know that you may need to explore values for change or work on increasing confidence over a few conversations.

Change Talk
Drs. Miller and Rollnick (2012), state change talk occurs when an individual starts to use language indicative of the desire to move toward change. Change talk consists of self-motivational phrases used by an individual showing that he or she is actively thinking about making a change, and is currently considering the change from various angles. Change talk occurs mainly within the realm of four specific contexts: *desire, ability, reason and need.* In their book, Helping People Change, Miller and Rollnick describe change talk as follows:

Desire: **I want, like, wish...**
When an individual uses statements about what he or she wants, would like, or wishes for, he or she is using change talk related to *desire*. This person is expressing his or her desire to resolve ambivalence and make a change.

Ability: **Can, could, able...**
When phrases about what an individual can do, could do, or is able to do are used, these phrases are change talk related to *ability*—that is, the individual is pausing to consider what he or she is capable of with regard to change, which indicates that he or she is on the path to making that change.

Reason: (for this reason...)

Every time a person starts exploring reasons to make a change, this is *reason*-related change talk. This form of change talk indicates that the person making these statements is giving consideration to various reasons that a potential change would be a good thing.

Need: Have to, must, need...

When a person uses language expressing urgency in terms of "musts," he or she is using change talk related to *need*. This type of change talk shows that the individual feels compelled to make a change due to a sense that the change is no longer merely an option, but a necessity.

What influences change talk?

People become more apt to use change talk when they are given an arena in which to do so. You can facilitate this process (when appropriate) by being mindful of how you engage the individual you are working with during your conversation.

Encourage discussion of positives and negatives

By encouraging the ambivalent individual to talk about the good things about remaining in the status her to begin *planning* the change.

Explore extremes

While we are on the topic of exploring the positives of changing vs. staying the same, take it to the next level: ask the ambivalent individual about the best-case scenario if the change is made and ask about the worst-case scenario if he or she remains in the status quo. This gives an opportunity for the individual to consider the potential end result of his or her actions, which may help to propel the individual's desire to change and thus, lead to change talk.

Ask questions that are open-ended

When we ask open-ended questions (rather than "yes-or-no" questions, for example, or "either/or" questions), we open up a realm of possibility for the ambivalent individual. Open-ended questions give the individual a chance to think critically about his or her situation and how it might be improved by moving toward change. The idea behind using questions that are open-ended is to allow the individual to think for him or herself. If you think of the interplay between ambivalence and change as being akin to a maze, rather than pushing the individual toward a given answer by placing bait at the end of the maze (which is what is essentially occurring when we ask *closed*-ended questions), we encourage the individual to explore that maze and find his or her own way out of it by keeping the options for answers open.

Ask the individual to visualize the future

By asking the ambivalent person to consider the possibilities of the future—asking him or her to visualize the outcome if the situation he or she is in remains static, or to visualize the future after having made the change he or she is considering—you help to create a space for the person to really think about the impact that the change (or staying the same) would have on his or her life. By encouraging visualization, we encourage change talk—because if the person can see the possibility of a more vibrant future in which he or she thrives after having made the proposed change, he or she can begin to brainstorm on how to go about *making that change happen.*

The Action Plan

Once the ambivalent person—be it a client, a staff member, or yourself—has both assigned sufficient importance and built sufficient confidence, he or she is ready to make the next move toward enacting the desired change. How does one go about this? By creating an action plan that outlines specific things that the individual can do in order to bring the change from the realm of the sought-after and contemplated into the realm of reality.

The action plan should be controlled by the individual

The action plan should be autonomously constructed by the individual in question, rather than written up and given to him or her. An important part of enacting a behavioural change is taking responsibility for that change, and what better way to do this than by taking a very active role in planning and carrying out that change? Therefore, it is essential that the action plan be, for the most part, something which the individual has drawn up him or herself, without too much outside influence. Providing a general outline for the individual to fill in him or herself is fine, but try to stand back and let the person do the real work alone. Making your own action plan and carrying it out is a very empowering experience; it shows the individual that he or she has the know-how and ability to plot out and accomplish the goals outlined therein. This serves to reinforce the confidence to change—and, more generally, the individual's overall self-confidence.

The action plan should be manageable in scope
The action plan may set forth several different goals leading up to the ultimate behaviour change that the individual desires to make. However, each of these goals should be manageable in scope—no big feats, just a few things that are accomplishable. That isn't to say that the goals should be unchallenging and easy to achieve. On the contrary, a bit of challenge (although nothing too rigorous) can be inspiring. Rather, make sure that the goals being set are not unrealistic or out of reach. Setting unrealistic goals ultimately leads to disappointment and feelings of discouragement, whereas setting goals that are accomplishable serves to reinforce confidence by showing the person that yes, you *can* accomplish what you set out to do when you put your mind to it!

The action plan should be specific rather than general or broad
Rather than simply being a statement of the change that the person desires to make, the action plan should consist of smaller-scale goals that lead up to the ultimate goal of behavioural change. For example, if a person's desired behaviour change is to become employed and stop using public assistance programs, some goals that might be appropriate for his or her action plan would be, "applying to at least five jobs per week," or "using resume-polishing services to revamp my resume." The goals contained in the action plan should be related to and a part of the desired end result, but they should not be the end result itself. A castle is built in

small increments, and it is not built in a day. So too are bigger changes made— bit by bit, and over time.

Formulating the Action Plan

When creating the action plan, a good format to follow is the outline format: create lists of goals and questions related to those goals, and provide spaces for the answers. For example, creating a table with spaces for three specific goals (and a timeframe in which they shall be carried out) and what steps are going to be taken in order to accomplish them is a great place to start, as well as rating the confidence and importance levels of each of those goals using the trusty change ruler. Then, the individual who is making the change can expand further by writing down people who can offer support in accomplishing these goals (and in what ways they will provide support), potential obstacles to achieving the goals (and possible ways that these obstacles can be surmounted), and what specific results he or she expects to see in order to know that the action plan is working. Once these plans have been laid out on paper, the once-ambivalent person—you, your client or your staff member—is ready to spread those proverbial wings and take flight into the big open sky of actually enacting the change.

Strategies for Implementing the Four Steps

Now that we've discussed the four steps to resolving ambivalence in detail, you may be wondering how you can implement these steps with regard to your specific situation. In this chapter, we will explore a few stories outlining the strategies that are tailor-made for putting the four-step method to work for *you*.

Client-practitioner example
Lou's story,

21-year-old Lou was referred to me by the income assistance program. Lou was told he had one month of assistance benefits remaining before he would be cut off. Income assistance advised me that Lou needed to find a job immediately or his benefits would be terminated. When he came to see me, Lou was casually dressed and he seemed distant or removed. He gave me the impression that he was unconcerned that he was about to lose his sole source of income—income he needed to pay for rent, food or other essentials. Lou appeared to have all the time in the world, with no obvious sense of urgency given his predicament.

I began the conversation by building rapport and asked Lou to tell me a bit about himself. He said there wasn't much to tell. I gave my best effort to build rapport, as I knew without rapport I would be like a person in a canoe with only one oar in the water, only able to paddle one side of the craft. Basically, I knew without rapport our conversation would go in circles. Determined to go slow in order to go fast, I stayed the course and decided to take a different approach to engagement. I asked Lou if he wanted to be here; more specifically, did he want support in finding employment. He said, "nope—not at all." With that out of the way, I was able to determine that Lou likely had low importance for change—or, at least, that this was a distinct possibility. I had two choices: I could ask him what would make it more important to him to stay and hope that he would find some value in our time together... or let him go.

I think that as practitioners we have to be willing to let go, and to trust that when it makes sense for the person to be with you he or she will—but if there is no readiness for change, we can't install motivation. We can only pull out what already exists. Not an easy pill to swallow, I know. That "righting reflex" pulls at us to try harder, to do everything in our power to help a client better him or herself—but this is a fallacy. We cannot assist those who are not ready to be assisted.

For some clients, it is almost as if they no longer have a story to tell. In some ways hope has died. When I find myself in this type of scenario, I choose compassion and acceptance. I won't judge someone for the choice he or she is making today, and I have to trust that if I provided the best environment for that person to connect with me and they still choose to say no, I must accept it and ultimately move on. This was the case with Lou.

Organization-or-department-wide change (new computer/software, etc.)

Mary's story,

Mary works in payroll for a fairly large organization, and has been with the company for seven years. The organization experienced a fair amount of turnover in the first four years of Mary working there. The company has had new leadership in place for the past three years, and they have also moved to a bigger office, and all staff has been given new desks and chairs. The staff remark on how professional the office now looks and appreciate that leadership has invested in quality chairs and work stations for them.

Mary's supervisor recently expressed how saddened he was by Mary's lack of support for the new computer system they now use. A system he described as being less complex than the old one, as well as being linked to other departments to allow for more efficient work for everyone. Her supervisor shared that they were concerned that Mary may eventually lose her job if she didn't step up, as her output was now considerably slower than new hires who just started with the company—the very opposite of her past performance. Her supervisor explained that Mary is doing everything in her power to influence staff that their new computer system is ineffective and will make their jobs harder. Her supervisor also said that Mary is quite vocal in the lunch room, advising others in the department that if payroll staff don't voice their concerns now they will all be in trouble come year end.

Mary's supervisor asked if I would speak with her, as he values her—and so do the others in his department. He was concerned that Mary and his whole department were divided; the company worked hard to build a positive culture, which was something Mary had contributed to for the past seven years. Leadership didn't want to see Mary go. However, they also expressed that she couldn't keep the department from moving forward any longer.

When I met with Mary I walked through the Four Steps with her.

Step 1: I asked Mary to share the benefits of not using the new system. She stated that she felt comfortable with the old system—that it worked fine, and she was able to do what she had to do in five easy steps. I empathized with her and expressed accurate understanding by stating that she took a complex process and broke it down in a way that seemed simple to her. Then, I asked her if there were any other good things about the old system. Mary stated that with the old system she was responsible for training all the new hires on the system and she felt she had significance with the company because the new staff respected her knowledge. Again, I voiced how she felt special and was given the privilege of training people for the payroll department, and I also reflected how she got to influence the positive culture she has enjoyed for the last seven years.

While it could have been tempting to advise Mary to move on—since the past system wasn't coming back, and her job was now at risk—I knew this would not be helpful. As much as I felt Mary needed to move on, I knew she needed to *see* that she needed to move on and embrace the system because she *wanted* to and not because she was *forced* to.

I asked Mary if there were any other reasons to stick with the old system. She said that was all she could think of, so it was time to move on to the next step in the process.

Step 2: I asked Mary if she could share any reasons to embrace the new system. She paused for a long time before finally sharing one: she stated one reason to use the new system was so she would be more efficient. I asked her to tell me more. She explained that she was living in two worlds, that she partially used the old system and methods while simultaneously using some of the new methods. She noted that working in both systems was taking her a significant amount of time; she sounded regretful as she added that while she used to be the fastest at imputing information into the computer, she was now the slowest one in the department. After a long pause, she added that she was embarrassed and said she felt like she was a poor employee. It was evident that Mary was quite sad; her jaw quivered and she kept her face down.

In an effort to go beneath the iceberg, I asked if she could share *why* it was important for her to be more efficient at work. While we, as facilitators, may *think* we know the answer to this question, we need to remember to keep our assumptions firmly in place. Keeping in mind that everyone has their own values that influence change, we must take the time to find out theirs and keep your own values as far out of the conversation as possible.

Mary shared that she felt proud when her supervisor highlighted her skill and speed as an example to new hires. I reflected back how she valued being a model employee and doing quality work and how she is now feeling like the student in a time-out chair because she wasn't embracing the new system. She said that was exactly how she felt—she felt like she was in trouble, and that her supervisor now only saw her as a bad employee like the people that used to work there. Mary voiced that she thinks her supervisor has forgotten that she was one of the "best employees ever" and now only saw her as a trouble-maker, and one who was less efficient.

Remember that empathy follows at every step. Essentially, my aim is to hold a mirror up for Mary to see and hear what her heart is saying and feeling. I offered that while she is hesitant about the new system, she clearly values doing good work and supporting a positive culture. I focus now only on her reasons to change and why each reason is important to her. I also reflect all the reasons, desires, needs and abilities to move forward as she expresses them to me. I also gently highlight the discrepancy between Mary's value to work in a positive culture and her reluctance to support the new system.

At this point in the conversation, I would say Mary was about a five on the ruler of readiness for behaviour change. She was given the opportunity to express the good reasons for not fully adopting the new system; while discussing the benefits of not changing she would have been at a zero on the ruler. When I asked her what the good things were about using the new system, she moved off the zero mark on the ruler and began to shift towards behaviour change. At this point in the conversation, it's important to stay empathic and focused so that we don't inadvertently move back down the ruler. My focus is to move Mary forward. Should Mary speak about the good things of the old system, I will acknowledge and not dismiss what she said—I will not however, linger there. I am staying focused on moving up the ruler, and while I have empathy for Mary's situation, I simply am mindful of the direction we are moving in, and making sure that direction is *towards* behaviour change.

Step 3: To transition from Step 2, I summarized what Mary has shared thus far. I acknowledged that while Mary saw some benefits to not embrace the new system, those reasons didn't quite match up with who she is as person. I offered that she wants to continue to nurture the positive culture that she works in and she knows that in order to do so, she must let go of the old system so that she can be more efficient—something that is important to her.

At this time, I shifted the focus of the conversation by asking if we could discuss her confidence in her ability to move forward with this new system. She said she would appreciate that and warned that she doesn't think it will be an easy process for her. She commented how "it's not easy to teach an old dog new tricks!" Once again, I empathized by reflecting that while she is willing to move forward, it won't be easy—but the willingness to move on is present.

I asked Mary to take a step back and asked if she can recall times in the past where she had to make a change and—while it wasn't easy—she did it. After a long pause, Mary said a couple of things came to her: one was quitting smoking and the other was losing a significant amount of weight. She said that quitting smoking was one of the hardest things she had ever done, and if she could get through that she probably could make it through anything. She also shared that at one time her diabetes was out of control, and—tired of living a life of insulin dependency—she said she got serious about her health and lost almost 70 pounds and had maintained that weight loss now for almost a year. When I congratulated her on her focus and determination, she teared up and shared that while the last few years had been hard, she has never felt better about herself—until recently, that is. Before the new system at work came along, she finally felt like she was living the life she always imagined. Now, she feels awful at the end of the day and wonders if she will even have a job to go to if she doesn't learn this new system soon. She said she wished she would have figured it out at the beginning, as now she wondered if her supervisor had given up on her, and if there was even any point in trying.

I summarized Mary's past successes and her desire to continue working for the company where she was once held in high esteem. I also reflected that she had been successful in the past and how she wanted this success again, and that when she put her mind to something not a lot could stop her. She said she agreed, and said her family thinks she is like a race horse: when she wants something, she will do whatever it takes to get it.

Continuing with her positive momentum, I affirmed that she is determined, and I asked what other strengths she felt she had. She shared that she normally is a quick learner and has the ability to perform a task once seeing it done a number of times. Once again I affirmed her ability to manage both the old system and the new one—and while it wasn't as efficient as she would have liked, she had found a way to make it work for her over the last few months. I also reflected how she was able to learn how to be proficient with the old system—one that was viewed as complex—to the extent that she had been able to break it down into a few manageable steps.

After exploring Mary's past successes and strengths, I asked her how confident she was (on a scale of zero to 10) that she could let go of the old system and learn to fully use the new system within the next month. She replied that she was about a four. When I asked what could *increase* her confidence slightly—say, to a five or six—she said she would need to know that her supervisor wasn't pressuring her to learn everything in one day. I asked her what else she needed to increase her confidence, and she said she needed to know that eventually the learning would end and that she would once again be proficient like she was on the old system. I continued to unpack what Mary needs to increase her confidence in her ability to adapt the new system, thus helping her to normalize her needs.

Once we exhausted her list of what she needs to increase confidence, I asked her why she rates herself at a four on the confidence ruler, and not a one or even a zero. Mary stated that she is at a four because she has learned many new things through her years and she could do it again if she had to. After thoroughly exploring why she rated herself higher, I moved on to creating a neuro-pathway.

To create a neuro-pathway for using this new system fully, I asked Mary to envision herself six months from now *successfully* using the system, and asked her to break down the steps she thinks she had to take to get to this wonderful place. As she broke down the steps, I contributed other ideas for her to consider as well.

Lastly, I asked Mary who could support her in fully integrating the new system. She noted that she could ask some of the ladies she trusts in her department who won't give her a hard time about asking. She also added that she could ask people she knows who struggled with the change like she did, but have now moved forward and fully adapted to the new system.

By this point, Mary was well on her way to the end of the ruler of behaviour change. Mary had used extensive change talk in Step 3, indicating that she may be ready to move on to the next step. Now, it was time to check in to see if Mary is ready to make a commitment to change.

Step 4: I asked Mary, "What is one small thing you would be willing to try in order to move towards implementing this new system fully?" Mary replied that she just has to *do* it, she has to let go of the old system and if she doesn't start now, she will simply prolong the inevitable. Prompting her once again, I asked what she intended to do first. She stated that tomorrow morning, she will not open the old system's program up at all, and will work only in the new system—regardless of how slow she feels she is. She stated that she is determined to lick this thing! Armed with a plan of action and some ideas for how she can find support in her goal of adapting to the changes in the workplace, Mary became ready to initiate changes to her behaviour at last.

Mary's story is quite common. It is not unusual for a workplace to implement new systems or processes—after all, we are working in the 21st century, where organizational change is the norm. Yesterday's way of doing things may no longer be an option tomorrow. The best support we can offer Mary or those who find themselves in today's ever-changing workplace is that of *choice*. If someone is in a situation where he or she is resisting the latest change, remember that as leaders, we have options. While these options may not feel as natural to *us* as fixing problems or doling out advice, they will be treasured by those on the receiving end. By providing tangible support where an individual can *choose* to embrace the new without judgment, we can change the environment of resistance to one of curiosity and openness. We hope you will give it a try!

Personal change
Roxanne's story,

I have been fortunate enough to have had participants in my training courses explore *my* ambivalence as part of their learning. For years, I myself struggled with ambivalence regarding exercise. If you looked at my outward appearance, you would see a physically fit woman who takes care of her health—when in fact, I would rather have lit my hair on fire than exercise. At one point in my life that was the case... until one group I was working with changed everything.

The group—who was pivotal in resolving my ambivalence about exercise—went through the Four Steps with me. They were as natural as ducks taking to water; they were patient and they trusted in the process, not allowing their shaky confidence in their newly-acquired and as of yet undeveloped skills to interfere with their determination to see the process in action.

I should mention that I had often used my ambivalence toward exercise as an example for my participants to practice their newfound skills. What was different with this specific group was their honoring of the status quo, or understanding that there must have been *some* good reason to not change or I wouldn't have brought up the topic. They came with curiosity and patience rather than being focused on an agenda to move me up the change ruler in order to carry the title of "the group who finally moved Roxanne forward."

When they asked me what the benefits of *not* exercising were, I responded with my typical, "I don't have to get sweaty!" Most times, participants quickly move on to exploring the benefits of exercise and never think twice about digging further into the reasons for remaining in the status quo. A common error participants and practitioners make is letting their eagerness rule—they want to get to where they are going instead of patiently trusting that the person knows him or herself best . The individual is in need of a guide—not a military official—to provide support on his or her journey through the clouds of ambivalence.

This group modeled great patience, asking me to take a step back and think really hard about what would be good about never exercising at all. Then they just paused... a long pause. I was able to really dig deep and think about what would be good about never exercising, ever. After several minutes of thought, I got it. I finally had that moment I craved for years. You see, I never really knew why I didn't exercise—I just knew it was something I avoided and there must have been a good reason for it, because I avoided it like someone who runs from the plague!

My jaw began to quiver and a lump formed in my throat as I sat with my understanding of why I avoided something that I, in fact, desired. You see, one of my deeply-held values is that of living a long and healthy life. I also understood that in order to live that long and healthy life, I needed to exercise. Let me offer some context around this value: I began my parenting journey at age 20, and while my beautiful daughter was a precious gift, I knew my life was about to change drastically—and it did. A couple of years later, my son followed and later, another daughter. By the

51

time I was 25 years old, I was married and had three children. Having a family so young certainly had its advantages, and today I am reaping the rewards as I pursue the things I had on hold in my early days. Now that I am empty nester, I want to be strong and healthy so that I can *do* the things I imagined when I was in my early 30s. In order to achieve the dreams I have carried since I was a young mother, I need physical strength—and that doesn't come from refusing to take the stairs to the first floor of a building.

As you can see, I had a dilemma. I avoided anything to do with exercise, even as I carried the inner desire to be physically strong. This amounted to a big, ugly discrepancy between behaviour and values. Sitting in the "client chair," I was able to feel that familiar discomfort, as I always did every time I used my story of exercise ambivalence in my trainings. The unfortunate part was that I had never been able to move forward. What I *did* walk away with were many ideas on how I could start exercising. People loaded me up with ideas as if I couldn't find them for myself, with participants offering suggestions like using the Bowflex, or running, lifting weights and other activities that others thought I should begin immediately in order to build my physical strength up.

What people had always missed was I didn't *need* the ideas, I needed to understand *why* I didn't do what I so *wanted* to do. It was shameful to live with this discrepancy, and the fact that I never followed through week after week just increased my embarrassment. When sharing my story in trainings, I would nod my head and thank the participants for their ideas. I also reminded them that they were in fact sharing things that I might be familiar with, or at the very least I could find on Google myself. They seemed to understand that they had missed something, yet that desire to "fix" or find the perfect solution drove them forward, regardless of my feedback.

This group, as I mentioned previously, was different. They stayed the course—and I realized *why* I avoided the stairs and anything that involved any type of physical exertion (including vacuuming and housework). Just kidding about that one! Actually, I managed the housework, but barely;

after cleaning I found myself taking pain relievers like ibuprofen to deal with the headaches and back spasms. You might think that I would be able to clue-in that exercise meant pain. The entire time that I thought I was avoiding exercise, when in fact, I was avoiding *pain*. All those years I completely missed the obvious: it was never about not wanting to exercise, it was about avoiding what followed—the pain.

I told my participants in the training that one of the benefits of never exercising would be not having to live with the pain that followed. Of course, they didn't get it. But *I* finally did—and it was big. It was my "a-ha!" moment, it was the light at the end of the tunnel for me. In fact, I didn't want to continue with the Four Steps, because I didn't need to. All this time, all I needed was to understand and resolve my ambivalence and I had.

Many years ago, I was in a terrible car accident that involved months of physical therapy. The therapy itself was grueling, and afterward I was always in horrific pain. To deal with the pain, I took medication. Fortunately, my pain medication wasn't of the prescription variety—if it had been, I am sure I would have been become addicted to pain medication. The only saving grace for me was my knowledge of how addiction works, knowledge that came from my training as an addictions counselor. My way of avoiding the addictive pain medication (and thus, avoiding addiction itself) was essentially avoiding exercise; as a result my back was weak and couldn't support any type of physical activity. The bottom line is that I avoided what I wanted, without understanding *why* I was ambivalent about exercising, and thus did I remain caught up in a cycle of embarrassment and disappointment.

In our debriefing, the participants within the group were able to experience what it felt like to guide someone through (and experience their own) "a-ha!" moment. They were able to see someone have a breakthrough without having to come up with all the solutions. Many shared that they found constantly problem-solving for all their clients exhausting—day after day, they would prescribe a solid action plan, only to see their clients not follow through. They were discouraged and frustrated and so were their clients.

Maintenance After the Change

Moving out of the swamp of ambivalence and making a firm commitment to make a change is a commendable feat—but it doesn't end there. Although change can at first be exciting and refreshing, over time there can sometimes be a tendency to relapse into old ways of behaving. In this chapter, we would like to discuss the steps that can be taken to *maintain* the change that has been made, making the short-term victory over ambivalence into a long-term success story.

External supports provide that little extra bit of encouragement that a person needs in order to complete his or her journey to change. Often clients have little to no support system in their lives—their socialization may have been limited to interacting with people who were not supportive of their desire to change, or who behaved in ways that would impede their ability to change. Take the time to build supports into the plan. For some people they may feel alone now that they have transitioned into the change they desired. Encourage people to find and build new connections—connections that are conducive to maintaining the changes that have been made.

First, encourage autonomy by asking the person what ideas he or she has for ways to build up a solid support system. Then share some ideas of your own (don't be afraid to be creative with your ideas). Some ideas I have heard in the past are joining a book club, volunteering with an organization or for a cause that the person holds dear, going back to school and even moving into a new neighborhood. All of these things can bring a fresh start, a new beginning, and serve to encourage the forging of new friendships with people who are likely to be supportive of the new, changed person that the client has become.

Another important aspect of maintenance after making a behaviour change is having effective coping strategies in place that the person can turn to in times of need. The temptation to relapse into old ways of behaving will undoubtedly pop up at some point, so it is crucial that the individual who is working to solidify the change he or she had made have some ideas for ways to deal with the feelings that arise when the temptation to backslide beckons. Again, ask the individual for his or her input on what sorts of coping mechanisms he or she can use in the face of temptation to backslide and then offer ideas of your own. Coping strategies may be as simple as vowing to chew gum when the temptation to smoke cigarettes arises, or as complex as an elaborate meditative exercise when feeling overwhelmed by stress. Predicting potential moments of weakness of resolve and planning ahead to manage those moments is pivotal in keeping temptation in check and strengthening the individual's resolve to maintain the change that has been made.

Transition is a process

In his book, *Managing Transitions*, author and organizational change consultant William Bridges wrote that change is a tangible, physical thing that takes place. Everyone can see it, and everyone must adapt to it. The *transition*, however, is a psychological thing, and is something that each person involved in the change must come to grips with for him or herself. The change is the "what," but the transition is the "how." In many ways, coping with transition after a change has been made can be akin to mourning: one must let go of the past, flounder a while in the unknown and uncertain, and finally come out on the other side with hope for a better future after the change. Although Bridges applied his philosophy on change and transition to a corporate environment, it is also applicable for *any* person learning to cope with a change—whether the change was mandated or self-propelled, there is always a time of adjustment, and there are things that can be done to make this adjustment more smooth and less traumatizing.

Bridges (2009) offered a framework for leaders to guide their staff and clients through transition:

> First, staff must let go of the old ways and the old identity people had. This first phase of transition is an ending, and the time when leadership need to help people deal with their losses. Second is going through the in-between time

when the old way is gone but the new isn't fully implemented. Lastly, the coming out of the transition phase is when a new beginning emerges. This is when people develop a new identity, they experience new energy, and discover new sense of purpose.

These authors offered different starting points for creating readiness to change and offered no consistent model to follow. The key piece here is the *readiness* of staff and clients. Success depends on the readiness of the ambivalent individuals to put the old ways of doing things behind them, including the identities they got from the methods they used before—the methods that do not line up with their values.

In today's rapidly-changing world, people must be able to change rapidly themselves to keep up with the fast pace that life so often takes. All organizations and people go through change, whether by choice or with no other available option but to change, where they are essentially being backed into the corner. What makes organizations and practitioners highly effective at managing change is their knowledge of how to guide people through change effectively.

Take the time to explore what meaning the status quo has to a person, or the identity that a person draws from not changing (e.g. Step 1—exploring the benefits of not changing) and remember that because making the change is new for them, they need to envision what the new change will look like. If the individual's identity is tied into being the best at using the old system, by asking him or her to change you are, in essence, asking this person to give up his or her identity and sense of competency. Unless you offer support and acknowledge the courage it takes to make the leap from the old identity, you may find your words of encouragement—or worse, your threats—are ineffective.

Relapse is a distinct possibility—but it's *not* the end of the world
The best way to handle a relapse into the old way of behaving, or recycling (where a regression into an earlier stage of the change process takes place) is not with disapproval or a feeling of having failed, but rather

as *normal*. No one on this earth is perfect, and change is a dynamic process, not a static and unmoving entity. As such, relapses are to be expected. They, too, are a part of the change process—and they serve to cement the behavioural change when they are dealt with appropriately. The best thing that we can do when we relapse or recycle is to learn from our experience. What worked? What didn't? Evaluate the instance of relapsing or recycling and ask what the take-away message could be.

Often, people relapse in an attempt to seek old comforts when they find themselves in new, uncomfortable territory—and the process of change can be quite uncomfortable at first! Yet often, they find that the comfort they sought in returning to old behaviours is very limited, very finite. For example, a person addicted to drugs might relapse and go on a binge, giving up his or her quest for abstinence in favor of a drug high. However, the high does not last forever and the person may feel quite dejected for having shrugged off his or her recovery for a temporary lift. The crash after the high and the feelings of shame that may arise from giving up a good chunk of time in recovery.

Sometimes, the disappointment—whether in the relapse experience itself, or in oneself for giving in to temptation, or a combination of both factors—can serve as a motivator to get back onto the right track. So, rather than viewing relapsing and recycling as a negative event, it is important to view it in a more neutral light and to squeeze what positives you can out of it. It isn't a failure of the process—it is *part* of the process.

Teaching a man to fish
There is an old proverb that says, "give a man fish and it feeds him for a day; teach a man to fish and it feeds him for a lifetime." By reading this book and exploring the swamp of ambivalence—and learning how to work your way out of it using the four-step method described within these pages—you are learning to fish. Perhaps you bought this book with a specific situation in mind, some particular instance of ambivalence that you (or someone you work with) needed help working through. However, now that you have worked your way through the steps to the end result, you can apply what you have learned in the future. Life is full of

uncertainty, and thus, full of moments where we feel torn between two options. What you have learned here can accompany you as you go forward, and you can pass it on to others who may be feeling stuck in the swamp. You can be their navigator. You can guide them through the steps so that they, too, can feel more confident in making decisions to change. In so doing, you are passing along the fishing pole and helping others to become capable of helping themselves.

Conclusion

I sincerely thank you for purchasing and reading this book. I hope that you found it helpful in your quest to resolve ambivalence—be it ambivalence that you were experiencing personally, or ambivalence that those you work with are going through.

As we move along on life's path, we are presented with many forks in the road. If only these forks were easy to choose between—with one being dark and ominous, and the other brightly-lit and inviting—then books like this one wouldn't be necessary! The advice would be summed up neatly in one sentence: always choose the brighter path.

Unfortunately, in our real lives, choosing between the two forks in the road—choosing between two options—isn't nearly so easy. In most cases, there are benefits and drawbacks to either option, and sometimes we simply want to stick with what is familiar out of fear of the unknown... even when the unknown path leads to something better.

Lastly my hope is that this book, When *they* Choose Change will serve as a compass for you, helping to point you or those you work with in the right direction: the direction of learning to autonomously choose change and resolve ambivalence. I also hope this book has helped you to reconsider your perception of change and ambivalence, so that you may view it—not as a negative thing, but as something to be embraced, worked through, and utilized to its fullest capacity in order to make your life or the lives of those you work with better.

About the Author

Roxanne Sawatzky lives on beautiful Vancouver Island, Canada, with her biggest champion – her husband. She has always been a passionate advocate for those don't have a voice, especially those who are vulnerable and experience multi-barriers to employment. She provides training and consultation to organizations across Canada and Internationally. In her first research project she successfully managed a 3 year 1.3 million dollar research study for the Provincial and Federal Government with almost 3000 individuals participating. She is now completing her fourth research project using Motivational Interviewing as a model to support ambivalent individuals move forward. Roxanne has done workshops and presentations nationally and internationally. She has completed her M.A. Leadership and Organizational Change, she also holds a certificate in addictions counselling and case management. In addition, Roxanne became a member of the Motivational Interviewing Network of Trainers in Spain in June 2009.

About the Editor

Tamara VanWormer lives in sunny southern California, on the cusp of the United States border with Mexico, with her wonderful husband and two darling children. She began her writing and editing career early in life, but put it on hold in order to obtain an education in the field of psychology and to work in the corporate world. She has now returned to pursuing her passion for the written word, and when she is not busy typing away at her desk, she can be found with her nose buried in a book or meditating in the mountains near her home.